This book is not for kids. This book is not for kids.

How do you make your girlfriend scream during sex?
Call and tell her about it.

How is a push-up bra like a bag of crisps?
As soon as you open it, you realise it's half empty.

What do boobs and toys have in common?
They were both originally made for kids, but daddies end up playing with them.

What do a woman and a bar have in common?
Liquor in the front, poker in the back.

What do women and noodles have in common?
Both wiggle when you eat them.

What do you get when you jingle a man's balls?
A white Christmas.

What's the difference between your boyfriend and a condom?
Condoms have evolved: They're not so thick and insensitive anymore.

What do you call the useless piece of skin on a dick?
The man.

What does a nearsighted gynaecologist and a puppy have in common?
Both have a wet nose.

Why did the woman leave her husband after he spent all their money on a penis enlarger?
She just couldn't take it any longer.

How does a woman scare their gynaecologist?
By becoming a ventriloquist.

What did the hurricane say to the coconut tree?
Hold on to your nuts, this ain't no ordinary blowjob.

How is sex like a game of poker?
If you have a great hand, you don't need a partner.

What's another name for a vagina?
The box a penis comes in.

What's the difference between anal and oral sex?
Oral sex makes your day. Anal makes your hole weak.

What did the penis say to the vagina?
Don't make me come in there!

What do you call a lesbian dinosaur?
Lick-a-lotta-puss.

What's the best part about sex with twenty eight year olds?
There are twenty of them.

What's the difference between a tire and 365 used condoms?
One's a Goodyear. The other's a great year.

Want to know why they say eating yoghurt and oysters will improve your sex life?
Because if you eat that stuff, you're sure to eat anything.

How do you circumcise a hillbilly?
Kick his sister in the jaw.

What's the difference between a woman with PMS and a terrorist?
You can negotiate with a terrorist.

What's the difference between a bitch and a whore?
A whore sleeps with everyone at the party. A bitch sleeps with everyone at the party—except you.

Why do women have orgasms?
Just another reason to moan, really.

What's the difference between your wife and your job?
After five years, your job will still suck.

How is tightrope walking like getting a blowjob from someone ugly?
If you want to enjoy either, you absolutely can't look down.

A woman walks out of the bathroom, winks at her husband and says, "I shaved down there; you know what that means."
The husband responds, "Yeah, the drain is clogged."

What did one of the prostitute's knees say to the other?
How come we spend so little time together?

What do you call two men fighting over a slut?
Tug-of-whore.

How is a woman like a road?
They both have manholes.

What do a bungee jump and a hooker have in common?
They're both cheap, fast, and if the rubber breaks, you're pretty much screwed.

Why did the snowman suddenly smile?
He could see the snowblower coming.

What's the difference between a clitoris and an iPhone?
Nothing! Every cunt's got one.

When is it okay to beat up a dwarf?
When he's standing next to your girlfriend saying that her hair smells nice.

What does a dumb slut say when you ask if she's ever tried 69?
"Thirty dudes is the most I can screw in one night."

How are women like linoleum floors?
If you lay 'em right the first time, you can walk all over them for the next 20 years or so.

How do you embarrass an archaeologist?
Give him a used tampon and ask him which period it came from.

What did the O say to the Q?
Dude, your dick's hanging out.

What do you call a smiling Roman soldier with a piece of hair stuck between his front teeth?
A glad-he-ate-her.

What do you call a herd of cows masturbating?
Beef strokin' off.

What do you call a guy with a small dick?
Just-in!

What do you call a guy with a giant dick?
Phil!

Why are men like diapers?
They're usually full of shit, but thankfully disposable.

What type of bird gives the best head?
A swallow.

What's better than a cold Bud?
A warm bush.

How did Burger King get Dairy Queen pregnant?
He forgot to wrap his whopper.

Why do walruses love a tupperware party?
They're always on the lookout for a tight seal.

Why do vegetarians give good head?
Because they're used to eating nuts.

What does one saggy boob say to the other saggy boob?
If we don't get some support, people will think we're nuts.

What's the best part about gardening?
Getting down and dirty with your hoes.

What did the banana say to the vibrator?
Why are you shaking? She's gonna eat me!

Why does Santa Claus have such a big sack?
He only comes once a year.

Why did God give men penises?
So they'd have at least one way to shut a woman up.

What's the difference between a Catholic priest and a zit?
A zit will wait until you're twelve before it comes on your face.

How do you catch a naked man that breaks into a church?
Catch him by the organ.

How do you get a nun pregnant?
Dress her up like an altar boy.

Why did Jesus die a virgin?
Every single "wound" he touched closed up.

What's the difference between a rabbi and a priest?
A rabbi cuts them off. A priest sucks them off.

What do priests and McDonald's have in common?
They both stick their meat in 10-year-old buns.

What did the sanitary napkin say to the fart?
You are the wind beneath my wings.

What do you call someone who refuses to fart in public?
A private tutor.

How is a girlfriend like a laxative?
They both irritate the shit out of you.

What did one butt cheek say to the other butt cheek?
"Together, we can stop this crap."

Did you hear about the constipated accountant?
He couldn't budget, so he had to work it out with a paper and pencil.

How is life like toilet paper?
You're either on a roll or taking shit from someone.

What do you get when you mix birth control and LSD?
A trip without kids.

What's the difference between your dick and a bonus check?
Someone's always willing to blow your bonus.

What's the difference between a pick-pocket and a peeping tom?
One snatches your watch. The other watches your snatch.

What do a penis and a Rubik's Cubes have in common?
The more you play with it, the harder it gets.

What's the difference between a pregnant woman and a lightbulb?
You can unscrew a lightbulb.

What do the Mafia and pussies have in common?
One slip of the tongue, and you're in deep shit.

Why does Dr. Pepper come in a bottle?
Because his wife died.

What does the sign on an out-of-business brothel say?
Beat it. We're closed.

Why was the guitar teacher arrested?
For fingering a minor.

What's the difference between a hooker and a drug dealer?
A hooker can wash her crack and resell it.

What is the difference between your wife and your job?
After five years your job still sucks.

Why isn't there a pregnant Barbie doll?
Ken came in a different box.

What does the receptionist say as you leave the sperm bank?
"Thank you for coming!"

What do you call a nanny with breast implants?
A faux-pair.

How is being in the military like getting a blowjob?
The closer you get to discharge, the better you feel.

What do you call a guy who cries when he masturbates?
A tearjerker.

Why does Miss Piggy douche with honey?
Because Kermit likes his pork sweet and sour.

What's the real definition of a male chauvinist pig?
A man who hates every bone in a woman's body—except his.

How are Kentucky Fried Chicken and a woman the same?
Once you take away the legs and the breasts you're left with one greasy box to put your bone in.

What's the best way to respond when a girl asks "what's up"?
"If I tell you, will you sit on it?"

What does it mean if a man remembers the colour of a woman's eyes after a first date?
She's got small tits.

What's long and hard and full of semen?
A submarine.

What do you call two jalapeños getting it on?
Fucking hot!

Why don't little girls fart?
They don't get assholes til they're married.

What do you do when your cat's dead?
Play with the neighbour's pussy instead.

What do you call an incestuous nephew?
An aunt-eater.

How do you embarrass an archaeologist?
Give him a used tampon and ask him which period it came from.

What's the difference between your job and a dead prostitute?
Your job still sucks!

What's the difference between hungry and horny?
Where you stick the cucumber.

What goes in hard and dry, but comes out soft and wet?
Gum!

Which sexual position produces the ugliest kids?
Ask your mum!

What do you call a smiling Roman soldier with a piece of hair stuck between his front teeth?
A glad-he-ate-her.

Why do women wear panties with flowers on them?
In loving memory of all the faces that have been buried there.

Want to hear a joke about my penis?
Nevermind. It's too long.

Why is sex like math?
You add a bed, subtract the clothes, divide the legs, and pray there's no multiplying.

A man and his family are staying at a hotel. The man asks the employee at the front desk if the adult channels are disabled.
No, it's just regular p*rn, you sick f*ck.

Why are hurricanes normally named after women?
When they come they're wild and wet, but when they go they take your house and car with them.

What's the difference between a woman with PMS and a terrorist?
You can negotiate with a terrorist.

One Liners
Please tell your tits to stop looking at my eyes.

Life is like a penis. Women make it hard for no reason.

Having sex in an elevator is wrong, on so many levels.

Your butt is nice but it would be nicer if it was on my lap.

Sex is like a burrito, don't unwrap or that baby's in your lap.

One day, a little boy wrote to Santa Clause, "Please send me a sister." Santa Clause wrote back, "Ok, send me your mother."

A woman participating in a survey was asked how she felt about condoms. She said, "Depends what's in it for me."

Life is like toilet paper, you're either on a roll or taking shit from some asshole.

The best way to make your wife scream during sex is to ring her up and tell her where you are.

Last week a girl asked me for sex. I had to disappoint her… so I said yes.

A family's driving behind a garbage truck when a dildo flies out and thumps against the windshield. Embarrassed, and trying to spare her young son's innocence, the mother turns around and says, "Don't worry, dear. That was just an insect." "Wow," the boy replies. "I'm surprised it could get off the ground with a cock like that!"

I went to a meeting yesterday at my premature ejaculators' support group. Turns out it's tomorrow.

Google is a woman because it doesn't let you finish a sentence before it makes suggestions.

I saw a dildo for sale described as "nine inches long and realistic." I thought: Which is it?

My mom thinks I`m gay, can you help me prove her wrong?

An Australian kiss – the same as a French kiss, but down under.

My neighbour has been mad at his wife for sunbathing nude. I personally am on the fence.

"Give it to me! Give it to me!" she yelled. "I'm so wet, give it to me now!" She could scream all she wanted, but I was keeping the umbrella.

A naked man broke into a church. The police chased him around and finally caught him by the organ.

I tried phone sex once, but the holes were too small.

A worm crawls out of a pile of spaghetti and says: "Damn, that was one hell of a gang bang!"

I'm not a weatherman, but you can expect a few more inches tonight.

Two deer walk out of a gay bar. One turns to the other and says: I can't believe I blew fifty bucks in there.

I asked my wife why she never blinked during foreplay. She said she didn't have time.

Limericks

There was an old man from Connaught.
Whose prick was remarkably short,
When he got into bed
The old woman said
"That's not a prick, it's a wart."

There once was a man from Devizes
Whose balls were of differing sizes
One was so small
You couldn't see it at all
The other so big it won prizes.

There once was a man from Leeds,
Who ate a packet of seeds,
Within the hour
His dick was flour
And his balls were covered in weeds.

There once was a Senator from Mass,
Who wanted a strange piece of ass,
He lucked up and found it
But screwed up and drowned it,
And now his future is past.

There once was a man from Nantucket
With a dick so long he could suck it.
He said with a grin
As he licked off his chin,
"If my ear was a c*nt I would fuck it"

There was a young lady from Brighton
Who had an incredibly tight 'un.
"Heavens Above!
It fits like a glove!"
"Oh! You ain't put it in the right 'un!"

That twisted ol' dude called Lee,
Had a thing for a woman's knee.
He tossed her a coin
She kicked in his groin,
And now he is known as Cicely.

That recently single dude Martin
Told his ex-wife "since our partin',
I've had women and men
Several geese and a hen
And a Hoover, and that's just for startin'"

There once was a man from China
Who wasn't a very good climber,
He slipped on a rock
And cut off his cock,
And now he has got a vagina.

Two lesbians north of the town
Made sixty nine love on the ground.
Their unbridled lust
Leaked out on the dust
And made so much mud that they drowned!

There once was a man from Sprocket
Who went for a ride in a rocket.
The rocket went bang
His balls went clang
And he found his dick in his pocket.

There once was a man named O'Doole
Who found some red spots on his tool.
His doctor a cynic
Said "get out of my clinic,
And wipe off that lipstick you fool!"

There once was a woman named Jill
Who swallowed an exploding pill.
They found her vagina
In North Carolina
And her tits in a tree in Brazil.

There once was a man from Bel Air
Who was doing his wife on the stair.
But the bannister broke
So he doubled his stroke,
And finished her off mid-air.

There once was a man named Keith
Who circumcised men with his teeth.
It was not for the leisure
Or the sensual pleasure,
But to get to the cheese underneath

There was a young man from Peru
Who fell asleep in his canoe.
While dreaming of venus
He played with his penis,
And woke up covered in goo.

There once was a fellow named Sweeny
Who spilled some Gin on his weenie.
Just to be couth
He added vermouth
And slipped his girlfriend a martini.

There once was a man from Pompeii
One day made a wife out of clay.
But the heat from his prick
Turned the clay into brick,
And tore all his foreskin away.

There was a young lady from Kew
Who said as the bishop withdrew.
"Oh the vicar is quicker
And thicker and slicker,
And four inches longer than you!"

There was a young maid from Madras
Who had a magnificent ass.
Not rounded and pink,
As you'd probably think;
It was grey, had long ears, and ate grass!

A young woman who came from Lahore
Would lie on a rug on the floor.
In a manner uncanny
She'd wiggle her fanny
And drain your balls dry to the core!

There was a young man named Bruno
Who said "fucking is one thing I do know.
Sheep are just fine,
And women divine,
But llamas are NUMERO UNO!"

There once was a man from kent
Whos dick was so long that it bent.
To save her some trouble
He folded it double,
And instead of coming he went!

There was a Young Lady of Norway,
Who casually sat in a doorway;
When the door squeezed her flat, she exclaimed, "What of that?"
This courageous Young Lady of Norway.

There was an old lady called Betty,
Whose armpits where hairy and sweaty,
She had a great knot,
In her stinky old twot,
And her pubes looked just like spaghetti.

There once was a man from Gosham,
Who took out his bollocks to wash 'em,
His wife said "Jack!,
If you don't put 'em back,
I'll stand on the bastards and squash 'em!".

There once was a man called Dave,
Who dug up a prostitutes grave,
She was mouldy as shit,
And missing a tit,
But look at the money he saved!

There was an old man from Harrow,
who tried to have sex with a sparrow,
the sparrow said "No,
you can't have a go,
as the hole in my arse is too narrow.

There was a young man from Newcastle,
Who could wrap himself up like a parcel,
And in that position, He did a rendition,
Of God Save the Queen through his arsehole

There was an old gal from Cape Cod
Who thought she was sleeping with God
But it was not The Almighty
With his hand up her nightie
It was Roger the lodger, the sod

There was an old whore pulling tricks
Who at one time could handle five dicks.
One day she did cry
Pulling out her glass eye,
Tell the boys I now can take six.

There was a young sailor named Bates
Who danced the fandango on skates.
But a fall on his cutlass
Has rendered him nutless,
And practically useless on dates.

There once was a man from Rangoon
Whose farts could be heard on the moon.
When least you'd expect 'em
They'd burst from his rectum
With the force of a raging typhoon.

A lady from South Carolina
Put fiddle strings 'cross her vagina.
With the proper sized cocks,
What was sex became Bach's
Toccata and Fugue in D Minor.

A newlywed couple named Kelly
Spent their honeymoon belly to belly
Because in their haste
They'd used library paste
Instead of petroleum jelly.

There once was a lady from Bude
Who went for a swim in the lake.
A man in a punt
Stuck his pole up her nose
And said "You can't swim here, it's too dangerous."

There was a young monk from Tibet
Who came up with the strangest thing yet:
His dong was so long
And so hard and so strong
He could bugger six yaks, en brochette.

There was an old whore from Azores
Whose pussy was covered in sores.
The dogs of the street
Wouldn't eat the green meat
That hung in festoons from her drawers.

KNOCK KNOCK...

Knock, knock. (Who's there?) Izzy Data. (Izzy Data who?) Izzy Data test tube in your pocket or are you just happy to see me?

Knock, knock. (Who's there?) A yam. (A yam who?) A yam so wet for you right now.

Knock, knock. (Who's there?) Amanda squeeze. (Amanda squeeze who?) You want amanda squeeze you all night?

Knock, knock. (Who's there?) Tara. (Tara who?) Tara McClosoff.

Knock, knock. (Who's there?) Someone. (Someone who?) Someone who will get you laid.

Knock, knock. (Who's there?) [Sexy voice:] Who would you like it to be?

Knock, knock. (Who's there?) Justin. (Justin who?) You're justin time to see me strip for you.

Knock, knock. (Who's there?) Ben. (Ben who?) Ben down and kiss my booty!

Knock, knock. (Who's there?) Ivanna Seymour. (Ivanna Seymour who?) Ivanna Seymour of you, naked.

Knock, knock. (Who's there?) Parton! (Parton who?) Parton my lips for you.

Knock, knock. (Who's there?) Ivana. (Ivana who?) Ivana kiss you all over.

Knock, knock. (Who's there?) Ivan. (Ivan who?) Ivan to do something naughty with you!

Knock, knock. (Who's there?) Anita! Anita who? Anita you right now!
Knock, knock. (Who's there?) Ida. (Ida who?) Ida rather be naked with you right now.
Knock, knock. (Who's there?) Dewey! (Dewey who?) Dewey have a condom handy?

Knock, knock. (Who's there?) Ida Comfort. (Ida Comfort who?) Ida comfort you a long time ago if I'd known how hot you are.

Knock, knock. (Who's there?) Al. (Al who?) Al let you touch my booty if you open this door.

Knock, knock. (Who's there?) Ben Hur. (Ben Hur who?) Ben hur over!

Knock, knock. (Who's there?) Iguana. (Iguana who?) Iguana feel you up, baby.

Knock, knock. (Who's there?) Ice cream. (Ice cream who?) Ice cream for you all night long.

Knock, knock. (Who's there?) Dozer. (Dozer who?) Dozer some great assets you got there.

Knock, knock. (Who's there?) Baby owl. (Baby owl who?) Baby owl see you later at my place.

Knock, knock. (Who's there?) Howie. (Howie who?) Howie gonna get freaky tonight?

Knock, knock. (Who's there?) Gladiator. (Gladiator who?) Gladiator during that threesome.

Knock, knock. (Who's there?) Boo. (Boo who?) Will you stop crying if I give you a kiss?

Knock, knock. (Who's there?) Orange. (Orange who?) Orange you glad this isn't actually a banana?

Knock, knock. (Who's there?) When where. (When where who?) Tonight, my place, you and me.

Knock, knock. (Who's there?) Do you want two CDs? (Do you want two CDs who?) Do you want to CDs nudes?

Knock, knock. (Who's there?) Jamaican. (Jamaican who?) Jamaican me horny.

Knock, knock. (Who's there?) Anita. (Anita who?) Anita you inside me.

Knock, knock. (Who's there?) Waiter. (Waiter who?) Just waiter I get my hands on you.

Knock, knock. (Who's there?) Baghdad. (Baghdad who?) I'd love to see you Baghdad ass up.

Knock, knock. (Who's there?) Disguise. (Disguise who?) Disguise your boyfriend? I can do you better.

Knock, knock. (Who's there?) Ike Anne. (Ike Anne who?) Ike Anne rock your world, baby.

Knock, knock. (Who's there?) Phil. (Phil who?) Phil McCrackin.

Knock, knock. (Who's there?) Orange. (Orange who?) Orange you excited to see me naked later?

Knock, knock. (Who's there?) Lisa. (Lisa who?) Lisa you could do is help me get these pants off.

Knock, knock. (Who's there?) King Yvonne. (King Yvonne who?) Kinky Von Kinkster, at your service.

Knock, knock. (Who's there?) Boss bank. (Boss bank who?) Boss bank you tonight if you're naughty.

This book is not for kids. This book is not for kids. This book is not for kids.
This book is not for kids. This book is not for kids. This book is not for kids.
This book is not for kids. This book is not for kids. This book is not for kids.
This book is not for kids. This book is not for kids. This book is not for kids.
This book is not for kids. This book is not for kids. This book is not for kids.
This book is not for kids. This book is not for kids. This book is not for kids.
This book is not for kids. This book is not for kids. This book is not for kids.
This book is not for kids. This book is not for kids. This book is not for kids.
This book is not for kids. This book is not for kids. This book is not for kids.
This book is not for kids. This book is not for kids. This book is not for kids.
This book is not for kids. This book is not for kids. This book is not for kids.
This book is not for kids. This book is not for kids. This book is not for kids.
This book is not for kids. This book is not for kids. This book is not for kids.
This book is not for kids. This book is not for kids. This book is not for kids.
This book is not for kids. This book is not for kids. This book is not for kids.
This book is not for kids. This book is not for kids. This book is not for kids.
This book is not for kids. This book is not for kids. This book is not for kids.
This book is not for kids. This book is not for kids. This book is not for kids.
This book is not for kids. This book is not for kids. This book is not for kids.
This book is not for kids. This book is not for kids. This book is not for kids.
This book is not for kids. This book is not for kids. This book is not for kids.
This book is not for kids. This book is not for kids. This book is not for kids.
This book is not for kids. This book is not for kids. This book is not for kids.
This book is not for kids. This book is not for kids. This book is not for kids.
This book is not for kids. This book is not for kids. This book is not for kids.
This book is not for kids. This book is not for kids. This book is not for kids.
This book is not for kids. This book is not for kids. This book is not for kids.
This book is not for kids. This book is not for kids. This book is not for kids.
This book is not for kids. This book is not for kids. This book is not for kids.
This book is not for kids. This book is not for kids. This book is not for kids.